Emotional Colors

Emotional Colors

MARVE HENDRY

CONTENTS

Hickory flicker bickering over creamy desires,
willing his will to flinch on benches of silky wood
wheeling woolens of filthy brainstormed thoughts
on blank pages…

alive, I am, to join all the frumpy dreadful peoples
shackled, shit-less, scorn of thorns padding my route
red carpets of blossomed yet now withered flowers
lay beneath my feet, tickling the freckles on my skin,
as I shake my Dalmatian-like spots
for the following hot pages…

~hopeful colors~

best kept secret~

if you fold your fingers
to the rugged lines
stretching out of your palm,
the fist you just molded
will guide you
through life's revolving doors.

keep everything
under lock and key
just like the *origami fist*
            that you see.

the famous dilemma~

the start of everything
begins with the end
of what's not meant to be,
giving rise to just about
                    anything

the door you close
behind you
will gently push
a window open,
allowing arrogance to sneak in,
killing any overrated modesty

I'm not a poet,
though appearances
could be deceiving;

if writing your thoughts
could be seen as poetry then
I am a poet
not yet a writer

if writing poetry
makes me one,
I might just be,
but then again
I'm neither

I'm not modest
nor do I embrace my self-sided arrogant self,

I am just like you
         but
    prouder.

how Buddha opened doors~

more than often,
the right itch
comes along,
tickling what you won't dare
to scratch;

patience is key
to opening doors
without touching any knobs

once in a while~

lives crisscross on every sidewalk
waving their auras around

unaware of each other's presence,
they fail to communicate
anything remotely pleasant

silence; their only sound

at that point, a word or two
is considered too profound

but once in a while,
light beads align
weaving a nexus
of magical serendipity.

paint your home with soul fingers~

green pastures
painted by hand
spilling their morning dew
to ponds nearby

   never too cold

just enough
to make my coffee mug
exhale pirouetting steams
as I witness
four seasons
in one afternoon;

come and see my year
 on a summer day.

~painful colors~

share my pain~

trace my veins
along rugged skin
and your pulse will beat
to every breath I take.

life's spell~

life makes it hard
to forget
when all you need
is a whiff
to remember.

never broken~

seldom do I care

willing myself
out of pits

dark, deep
abyss-like cravings

nothing to self-repair,

scares ironed out
yet imprints remain

my will, still strong
though my portrait has faded;
a blurry picture
in a worn-out wallet

my screams are dampened
by pride
while silence sleeps next to me
pillaging my dreams

I don't often share,
my secrets are mine;
a cancer marauding me softly

I feel them staring

stabbing me from all sides

when mornings come
I prepare for war,
paint and all,
safety off

most nights are painted with remorse
and yet
I would do it again
and again
and again
*for I will gladly suffer the wounds
of triumphant battles.*

I can't help myself~

I sit, there,
looking at the screen.
          I give up!

flipping through
the white noise
searching for a reason
not to scream,
nothing comes to mind

surrounded by his favorite toys
still scattered all around

the carpet stain
from that morning's spilled orange juice
now visible more than ever;
I witnessed it go darker and darker
I was there for all the shades

        he's dead
yet I still make his bed

I have yet to live a day
since the moment
he went away;
parts of me just stopped
and like a broken watch
     the rest followed.

our daily mirage~

maybe one day
I'll wake up from it all
and paint my ceiling
a dull rouge

blame it on drugs
or alcohol

pass the time
with loaded dice.
roll myself out of bed
for a change

look at the birds
in a different way

maybe one day
I'll see it all.
perhaps, I'll go swimming
in a waterless lake
and suddenly change
my life's pace

just maybe
but then again,
tomorrow is too tempting
*   to be passed away.*

when the worst meets the best~

my watch stopped
at 5 pm that day

she was gone

and I was stranded
behind the nursery's frosty glass-window
mumbling my agony
in dyslexic
yet jubilant tears.

waiting for strangers~

I had an emotion,
once.

a faraway devotion
to written words
and folded syllables
manifesting as vocal screeches
performed by a muted choir of "MEs"

I felt fearless
since my heart
was welded shut
from within

time blurs our meaningless moments
as we stumble through them
helpless and afraid

a fractured heart
is a ticking clock
with no snooze button
and yet I feel fine
rejuvenated,
a touch invigorated,
I feel fine

maybe I'm a fairy tale pretending
not to have a happy ending
just to avoid a child's laughter
and associated empathy

perhaps I'm a child
without parents.
definitely a parent without
a child,
yet I can still cry
yes I can still cry

surely, a child & a parent
waiting for that lonely door knock
wondering
will you ever come back,
if I begged on one more knee?

how children crawl and cry~

he rose on cushioned air
filling his lungs with warm words
willingly closing his eyes
for a second

a second that felt eternal
for an hour or two

she broke the jar
of inserted insults
as she shook it passionately
hoping for a savior to rattle out

meanwhile, kids stood still
on the edge of each room
contemplating poisonous fumes

air was a cancer
corroding them from within

the glass house
now stood chipped
from each end
as parents fought
and children crawled

they crawled to safety;
the safety of the unknown.

marriage bracelet~

I came close,

bounced playfully
on the edge

being yours
meant
I had to fall
willfully

pots and pans
thrown,

not wasted;

a melted roast
with time to spare

though scrubbed,
blood stains
still stand out
on white walls

we were stuck,
going forward backward
holding hands
through fist fights and feasts

kissing fire
with watered-down lips

it's the tongues
that sting the most

bringing men to their knees
and grown women
to inch-thick tears

      smile; the kids are here.

~confused colors~

the day my imagination stood still~

drunken thoughts
of deranged minds
mingle and prey

like an octopus reaching
through depths
of silent &
inky blackness

volcanoes stand
where viral pains
were eviscerated,

I'm here,
no longer awake,
thinking of me,
myself and the many
inside my wheeling brain

I'm here,
pushing the wheels of sanity

unmarked~

a man without a face
  I am,

a fully dressed wind
casting shadows
on past sins

breathing bruised blues
among Persian colors,

pushing phrases
  through worded seas

till my grave's reached

  without visitors
    or tears.

is that shoe yours or mine?~

dancing on pages
with aging pride
while life cheers me on
from the still steady stands

I'm not a poet,

I'm you,

writing words
with worn-down
rosy thorns.

~connected colors~

standing on a shrinking planet~

I shed my old
selfish shell
for a better me
to you

& found that every part forgone,
was a glimmering piece of me
waving goodbye.

ascetic echo~

I'm empty,
drained as beaches
in December,
wishing for summer

chained to seashells,
I drifted
only to twirl
with 10-feet tides.

paper and ink~

a complete surrender
of my blistering emotions;

one after the other
marching to the slaughter of verbs
and metaphors,

revealing the page,
that I slept on tonight,

still blank.

indigenous veins of turmoil~

saline serenades
wobbled their intricate notes
while gliding over my skin,
venting through flesh and cheekbones;

I cried

and felt the flux
of fluid ecstasy immersing
the scorn of compliments
delivered by stings of love, lust and
life's ironic lunacies.

I waved

goodbye to future promises,
tuning my strings for better tomorrows.

pearl-paved roads~

what is everything
but pearls of unconnected events
curling on a string,
weaving a necklace
around your neck;

beauty on display,
waiting to be broken back to pebbles,
bouncing their way
          to oblivion.

a beautiful day in hell~

frames without windows
disconnecting the yellow stains
of her bedroom,
blurring the shadows
of her projected dreams
        & memories

her landscapes are layered
with unspoken regrets
        replaying forever.

twilight variety~

whisper to the wind
twirling underneath our swollen wings
to convince the Gods of misfortune
that humanity's demise
is up for grabs.

breadcrumbs of regret~

      downstairs,
  amidst the crowds
rushing away from a slammed door,

  I stood motionless,
meditating our melodic
     melees and brawls.

bird of passage~

break the serene silence
over smothered clouds,

slide the rainbow's jingles
to push your sail of thoughts
and just
let the wind
blow you astray.

just before the void~

staring down
my life's barrel,
I remembered
how many times
 I giggled
        alone.

~emotional colors~

a battle of colors~

harvest the green
as blue moves away
framing black for purple's
foolish endeavors

colors keep changing,
intertwining through fabric
& skin

mirrors break
as if they refuse to lie
or tarnish the image,
once held by wiser women
                    & men.

colors change
and silence the wounds
like masters did
to unwilling slaves.

and then you wake up
feeling not as blue
nor as virtually-flawed,
not even fanatically clueless,
enjoying the brown &
wrinkled carpets of skin

welcoming-in
the unknown
the willing
and the flawless company

and there,
you plant the flag
of home,
dip your feet
in comfort's warmth,
hold the scars
of failed experiments

       & never let go.

Feel Your Colors~

an artist's painting
starts with his heart
red ink spilled from his blood
brush after brush, his tools turn grey

the master sits in front of his art
melancholy strikes, tears flood
silver eyes keep emotions at bay

as sad as one can be
he picks up his brush, in a rush
blue, is ready to gush!

stroke after stroke, fear is nowhere near
as he smiles, his brush begins to steer
ecstasy within, he plunges his tool
green!! the next frontier

that smile won't last, as yellow takes up fast
surprised, the poor devil sits back
admiring the drawings in his head

his hand trembles,
his brush, now in shambles
he dips in fear what only orange can appear
a master at work,
from the shadows, finally an outline is here

as his tune almost comes to an end
the angel knows his soul is fed
No!! shouts the poor devil
I'm not dead yet!!

as his anger boils
his rage comes through
he takes to the canvas
red, once true,
is splashed and dashed
upon his art.

the fool then smiles, so sad!
but wait!! what's that, hidden?
a new canvas,
shiny, silky white
there in the corner, arching on his stool
black, bloody red starts another fight.

pink on Baker-Miller street~

brand me a glitch
in a man's cocoon,
grasping for air
whilst graphite nails
erode away
in man-made coffins

I drank my own zeal
and pealed my inner Amaranth,
exposing seeds
of self-restraint
& a frail labyrinth

I'm bruised
on crocheted mattresses
licking magenta knuckles;

*naked, as mirrors are
          without you.*

I am blue~

i.
and so I fell in love
with a color;

a light-hearted hue
of aquamarine blue
that is often confused
with Cyan- infusions
or Azure-like brews.

ii.
I constantly found myself
embracing blue garbage bags
as I got ready to chase my neighbor's
celestial-blue Pontiac cruise.

iii.
I must admit
that blue nights,
more than once,
have blinded my misconceived rage;
red flames were found quenched
on shores of misconception
holding a blue flag
of my unconditional surrender

'tis true!
blue nights made me smile,
more than once.

iv.
and since blues were never cruel,
I had no choice;
I had to find dignity in loneliness
and unforgiven truths.

it's hard to rifle through
old blue folders and tiled packets
of memories & melodramatic scenes
past our prime and dignified hymns;

'tis hard but not impossible.

v.
soon, it became clear.
light is a craving of rainbows
amidst shades of villainous colors;
each with insignias of gullible bruises,
wishing they were *blue,*
                    just like me.

prismatic illusions~

please my senses
with divine intervention

while you dip your brush
in a bowl of sunlight
and paint the final lashes
on my broad scope
of lament words

I am yours to draw,
to smear every flaw and
break the lines
of a perfect snowflake
                    canvas

rewind my sins
in your movie of faith
and overthrown filth
till pain stops
and all that's left
is the right person
pressing play.

~seasonal colors~

amidst serenity and October skies~

the stairs
seemed endless
that day,
stretching my emotions
like cringing branches
pulled away from
nature's warmth

not a bird in-sight
maybe 'twas too cold
to sing.

I struggled
to puddle the ground
beneath me
with my wet scent &
misery

anathema of one's self
reverberated
to mirrored images
reflecting
what's missing from
printed portraits and
oiled-up paintings;
a moving target

she died,
he followed,
they disappeared &
I sighed

no tears

just a sad depiction
of a burrowed scarf
lost to winter's cruelty

red, velvety exterior
with mushy nostalgic innards

lost
without smiles,
or visitors,
vacant of any saline profusion

it was over

it took only minutes
to say goodbye
and a lifetime
to wave & welcome
them in & out
it was over
with fashionable black
and barbed eyelashes

they disappeared,

I sighed again

whispered my anguish
beneath my jades &
breaths

no one heard
but *they knew it was me.*

back when pancakes were found and not made~

~when leaves were
left scattered on fields
of frantic follies,
   she reached~

she reached
and dulled the damage
of villainous winds
rendering it
the tidiest of storms

she left crumb trails
of pure joy
& oven-baked feasts
for all to enjoy

filleted slices of family tales
and humorous settings
furnished the dining room
as her aura shone
through keyholes
& hinged crevices

now that the aromas

flowing in closed circuits~

current events migrate in flocks,

piggybacking their way
on wireless birds,
seeking shelter
among unaware herds

life has shifted through time

shoveling turd
from one ocean to another
as people swarm
on current trends
locking up live fun in clusters

like blue whales,
valued thoughts go extinct

all that's left
is algae-infested shores
mistaken for green meadows.

crimson shades of masochistic slippers~

trimmed edges of malignant and
power-shaded lipstick
vividly molesting the masses
as wealth trickled down in vain
to unsettled vases of egos
masquerading as brains.

follow me, my melody~

splashing water droplets
under grainy skies,
fluorescent critters
crawling under heaven's stars;

a trailing tail of purple dyes

as gods speak and billboards shine
majestic crickets sing
to dolphins' lullabies

doors crack open
to swallow the piper's tune
as mesmerizing maiden nymphs
color between the lines.

the journey's end~

the train ride to nowhere,
stopped midway

the ghost of her past stepped off
to meet and greet the passengers
from today's unfortunate friendships

the guests all ran
leaving nothing behind
but abandoned tracks
of once flourishing rails

she was left helpless
waiting for a ride
that never came

hope
burnt to ash,
packed and stocked in urns
upon shelves of regret

she saw herself
sinking in air

as she crawled to shore
alive but surprised,
she envied the dead.

let's not penetrate~

the dick-shaped bullets
        march onward
on fields of bloody glory;

a gory sight
of mankind's illness
stretches the entire
thorny battlefield.

scenes like these make me wonder;

if women ruled the earth,

would vagina-shaped ammunition
embrace rather than penetrate?

the irony in numbers~

why?
why would you willingly waver?

derailed dogma
looms over vengeful fists
and banged up coffee tables,
as if force could frighten
forceful monsters

trumpets of war
and grunge fables
took to the streets
mesmerizing the masses
to the hypnotic syllables
of hypocrisy

I'm surrounded
with twitching faces
racing to stitch their logos
on my brand new
 white polo shirt

–where are you now?
–selling drain cleaners
 to clogged-minded peoples

nights, now painted in haste,
bring hope with their lilac-white spots
faintly shining in blind corners

the why becomes why not!

until you realize that
they're only forgotten paint patches
left by the hidden
and the suspiciously invisible

and thus,
the why not becomes
why not earlier?

a taste of our own expired medicine~

light fades,
curtains dance
and jest
as they make an exit

he enters.

> –the room is not big enough
>   to hold egos like yours and
>   mine.

spectators turn left and right
as they hear the dialogue,
witnessing one simple silhouette
on both ends of
a dreaded conversation

(the conversation continues)

> –filter those feelings
>   through woolen rags
>   and give me back my dignity.

the room is emptied
then refilled
with rapid bursts and
outraged waves of
contempt, melancholy, despair
and an annoying dissatisfaction

~that feeling you get
when punching air
after a humiliating experience;
that time where
you froze, and gazed
with rage twirling
in your puppy eyes~

(the dialogue gets louder)

    –if dignity is sold in pairs,
     ours would be long gone by now
     with no self-esteem to spare

    –we are the sum
     of broken fractions
     multiplied to infinity
     and carried from one end to another
     under different flags and
     bottom lines. —take your rags back
     I have no dignity or feelings left; I'm as spent
     as a matador lying on a stretcher,
     moaning in pain.

the voices grow louder
and the masses huddle
and shout,
all united;
vengeance is in the air.

as anger festers,
darkness fades.
the crew, now scared,
keeps pulling the strings
of a panic-riddled stage.

the people are right,

two voices but only one man
or woman;
'tis still too dark to see.

a sexless shape
sipping its lines
with senseless emotions
and dry cinematic censorship
as if it's trying to stop time by boring it to death

light shines bright
and stars dangle
while mystique arises

and crowds cower
at the now-revealed figure.

–it's God.

and
he's tired of us.

& then I went outside
in search of blank pages
& opiate inks

Printed in Great Britain
by Amazon